Ty Cobb-
>Had a heart of a fighter,
>>That's why his play was brighter.

Mel Ott-

At the plate was always hot,

And kept hitting deep shots.

An early fog -
     Fish moving,
          While the night was improving.

A cat -

    Jumps out of bed,

        Too smell the flowers of red.

A cat -
Follows the river,
Feeling cold, it shivers.

A house -
    Has two dogs.
        And a massive old log.

A dog -
    Runs the in park,
        Then goes home at dark.

A piano -
>Doesn't play anymore,
>>Its keys are broken on the floor.

The small park -
    Empty on the rainy day,
        Everyone left on their way.

A park -
Closes at dark,
Even for the dogs that bark.

A cat -
		Sleeps in the door,
			Laying on the floor.

A dog -
>Runs in the yard,
>>And the house he'd guard.

A cat -

  Jumps out of a box,

    And Runs from the fox.

A boat -
Sails away in the night,
With the North Star shining bright.

A car -
> Races 110 on the road,
>> While driven in sport mode.

A car -
Passes another on the highway,
As it races on its way.

A river -
Runs to the lake below,
In a peaceful flow.

A river -
Crashes into the bay,
With birds resting on the shore of soft clay.

A departing sun -
	Leaves the sky in a glow,
		As away flies a crow.

A full moon -
    Night completely black,
        With shooting stars to track.

A summer moon-
        Cold fresh air,
                With a starry bright glare.

A cat-
Sleeps under stars of night,
Then leaves out of sight.

A dog -

Eats a steak,

Accidentally by mistake.

A frog-
		Jumps away,
			Doesn't want to stay.

A car-
          Broken by the telephone pole,
                    Still the person feels whole.

Willie Wells-
They called him the "Devil",
Because his game was top level.

A carnation-
    Red cluster of pedals,
        Shining like a gold metal.

A rusted cabin -
Tucked away in the trees,
The forest goer planting peas.

An old cabin-
        Built with massive logs,
                Now home to a few dogs.

The church-
    With Empty chairs,
        And quiet prayers.

A small island -
        Boats anchored in the sands,
                The speakers playing The Band.

A nighttime rain-
A wandering bird,
Sings a song unheard.

The little cat -
        Watches the man,
                Resting next to the fan.

A thick cat-
     Rests out of sight,
          Then plays thru the night.

The Marlboro -
It Burns out,
While a heart remains in doubt.

Red Wine-
    Accompanied by Loud Drunken songs,
        While the Night moves along.

The bus stop-
    One hobo waits for the bus,
        To go and meet his friend Gus.

The bus stop-
Has an ad,
With a lawyer looking glad.

A deer-
Peers from the side of the road,
Then quickly away he strode.

A bat-
      Goes quickly above,
            Racing a white dove.

Fish in the stream -
>Swim right pass,
>>As a cat watches from the grass.

Two deer -
        Jump out the way,
                Leaving as the skies turn gray.

A frog -

        Sits on the deck,

                Then jumps, landing in a wreck.

Thunder raging-
    Clouds of gray,
        The sun rushes away.

Clouds dark and gray-
        Slowly cover the mountain,
                Heavy Rains pour like a fountain.

Two Swans-
        Under the bridge they migrate,
                While a monk meditates.

A mocking bird-
        Hovering in place,
                With a smile on its face.

The house-
Put up for sale,
And Bought by a man named Dale.

Butterfly's-

      Dance in the park,

           After everyone left before dark.

A Butterfly-
      With Three spots of red and blue,
            Would go wherever the wind blew.

Departing Lovers-
        Leave each other,
                Their hearts were lost in the souther.

Hearts interlocked-
	The key not found,
		Yet the souls together bound.

Hands touch-
    A sensation felt,
        Two hearts melt.

Crimson Sunset-
 Clouds remain,
  Forecasting rain.

A Crescent moon-
Takes its place,
Above in outer space.

Fireworks-
  Rage in the sky,
    Scaring the birds that fly.

Fireworks-
>> Pop and scatter,
>>>> A loud patter.

A candle-
    Burns out,
        It's smoke, the only shout.

The maple tree-
     There sits an aged owl,
          His echoes a silent howl.

Five pines trees-
    One leaning down,
        The rest laughing at the clown.

Two cardinals-
        Drift out my view,
                In the sky of blue.

A blue jay-
Sits on the pole,
Then flys over the knoll.

A finch-
      Drinks from the pool,
            Then flies to nursery school.

A finch-
        Lands on the marbled fountain,
                Only to leave for the trees in the mountain.

A black night-

    With empty roads,

        Except for one loud toad.

A Peaceful stream-
One fisherman sits,
And his pole he fixes.

A small vly-
Two stray cats,
One fisherman wearing his lucky hat.

A cat-
Sleeps under the stars,
Dreaming about someplace far.

Violets-
    Purple, blue and white,
        For the eyes of night.

The mall-
        Filled on Friday,
                For the sales ending that day.

A coffee shop-
  Closes at seven,
    Sometimes at eleven.

A cat-
      Play with a ball,
            Ignores the owner's call.

The left fielder-
A power hitter,
Whose bat was bitter.

Old Colorado -
>   With mountains of green, and massive boulders,
>   Plus a skier with a broken shoulder .

Lilacs-
> Purple and soft,
>> Planted on the croft.

Lilacs-
    Of summer thrive,
        In the fresh air that's alive.

Lilacs-
      Dead in the courtyard,
            Now an image for a postcard.

An old Lighthouse-
    Decommissioned and neglected,
        As rust is now collected.

The Marina-
Peaceful nonetheless restless,
On this day when waves were crestless.

Waves-
        Crash and lapse,
                As boaters drink schnapps.

The Sun-
        Resting above the ocean,
                Stuck in constant motion.

Hoyt Wilhelm -
		Nicknamed "old sarge",
			Because of that fast baseball he'd discharge.

Bill Terry-
Played first base,
And hit homers into space.

Robin Roberts-
Pitched for the Phillies,
Who's curveball was chilly.

Claudio Monteverdi-
Composed music for all,
To be played in great halls.

Bobo Newsom-
>   His teammates called him buck,
>   And most games he had good luck.

The human hairpin-
Or Addie Joss,
Doesn't matter because his game had sauce.

Dock Ellis-
    Threw a no hitter on LSD,
        On June twelfth, for all to see.

Lefty Grove -
        A pitcher who hit some dingers,
                Who's fastball was certainly a singer.

Fifteen cats-
    Live in the barn,
        And play with yarn.

Yellow flowers-
    With a refreshing scent,
        That helps the soul vent.

Summer hay bales-
    Motionless in the distant,
        While the rains were persistent.

Hay bales-
Thrown in the air,
Brought to the fair.

Hay bales -
        Dried in the sun,
                Until sold to a farmer's grandson.

Daisies-
      Placed in a vase,
            Next the photos in the case.

Ancient Photos-
        Memories from the past,
                That stay and last.

Tulips of spring-
      Clouds dump cold rains,
            For the flowers to be picked for the lost lover's pain.

Three rose bushes -
    Bloom in early spring,
        As a mockingbird quietly sings.

An unspoken word -
    Was heard in a second,
        A prompt beckon.